How Cyber safe are you?

1. Are you active online?

2. Do you have online friends that you don't actually know in real life?

3. Do people you don't know keep wanting to be your online friend?

YES?

THEN YOU NEED TO READ THIS BOOK

How online safe are you?
TAKE THE QUIZ AT
THE END TO FIND OUT.

A note from the au
teachers.

I wrote this book for my children when they started to become active online. I quickly began to realise that they didn't really believe me when I told them that strangers online might not be who they say they are.

I was scared that my children were dangerously ill equipped to enter this new world, a world they simply had no defences for. I had myself been caught out by a very dangerous person I met online, so if I could be tricked what chance did they have?

It was obvious to me that children needed more help understanding and navigating the dangers and dangerous people lurking on the internet. That's why I ended up writing Robert the Lonely.

This story is a spine tingling and entertaining read for children, that will also help them to understand online stranger danger and hopefully help to keep them safe.

Don't miss the comprehension questionnaire on page 51. Encourage children to complete it, or use it to help facilitate discussions with your child about online safety.

ROBERT THE LONELY

ROBERT THE LONELY

Robert lived in a very large house on the top of a hill.
It was a very crooked house with crooked eaves and crooked roof tiles, and crooked windows and crooked doors. It even sat crookedly on top of the hill, which was also crooked.

The
outside walls
of the house
were very
very dirty and
black from
years of soot
and dirt. The
inside walls and the floors were also
black because the owners
had liked them that way
and Robert had never
changed them.
There were cobwebs
everywhere because,
although Robert was proud of his
house, he was not house proud and
besides, the house was too big for
Robert to clean all by himself.

2

Robert's huge house had ten bedrooms, three large living rooms, a huge kitchen, an enormous dining room, five bathrooms, an enormous creepy cellar and an even bigger and more creepy attic.

In every room dead flies, lying on their backs, with their crumpled legs sticking up in the air, lined the window ledges. Mouse droppings like chocolate sprinkles were scattered over the floors. Dust, as thick and heavy as ash, lined all the old gothic furniture.

Robert felt lucky to live in such a big old spooky house, but Robert was lonely.

Geoff

For a while Robert had lived in the house with a man called Geoff.

4

One day some men came for Geoff when he stopped moving anymore and began to smell.

Robert had been hiding in a dark corner when the men came and took Geoff away on a stretcher, pulling a sheet right over his head and saying something about hearts and attacks. After that, Robert never saw Geoff anymore, or anyone else for that matter, and that is why Robert was lonely.

At first Robert tried to distract himself from his loneliness by keeping busy, moving about from room to room. Sometimes he would count the dead flies on each windowsill. That would fill a few hours each day.

Sometimes to pass the time he would even try to catch the flies which weren't dead yet. Sometimes Robert liked to hang out in the kitchen, but it was quite draughty in there. Other times he hung out in the grand dining room, though it was a bit boring in there. Sometimes, for a change he would try the bathroom and sometimes even get in the bath but then, once he was in, he found it difficult to get out again. You know what it's like. Robert's favourite place to hang out though, was the sitting room, or living room as some people like to call it.

The living room was more cosy and less draughty than the other rooms in the house. This had been the room in which Geoff had spent

most of his time, and even though
Geoff was gone, he and the men who
had taken him had left the telly on, so
Robert liked to hang out in there
watching the various programmes
that came and went. Sometimes there
were even nature programmes about
insects and spiders, which he really
liked. He loved watching programmes
about spiders
especially.
They were
his
favourite.

Another   thing   that
had been left on after Geoff had
gone was the computer. Robert found
this out one day when he disturbed
the keyboard and the big screen in
front of it suddenly lit up.

Then a message flashed up on
the screen saying 'chat now.'

'Chat with who?' thought Robert, so
he pressed a few more buttons on the
keyboard and suddenly there
appeared lots of faces of children
filling the screen. Beside each face
and name was the instruction,

Chat to Joe...
online now!

Chat to Kayden...
online now!

Chat to Paris...
online now!

Chat to Mason...
online now!

Chat to Annie...
online now!

9

Chat to...

Well, you get the picture don't you?

Robert was amazed. He felt so alone in his big house but here were people in his living room at the touch of a button.

Suddenly, Kayden uploaded a goofy selfie and Robert couldn't help

KAYDEN

but laugh. He decided he really liked Kayden and would love nothing more than to be friends with him.

In fact, Robert wanted to be friends with all the children. They looked so happy and wonderful and alive. If he could at least be friends with some of them then he wouldn't feel so lonely would he? So, he pressed some more of the buttons, but instead of being able to chat with the children on screen as he had hoped, another message flashed up instead asking for his username and password.

"Bother," said Robert to himself. "What do I do now?" He'd never used a computer before, you see.

Just then some new words flashed up,

11

Not a member?
No problem,
you can sign up
here...

Robert clicked on the words and so began the process of signing up. Robert gave himself the username, 'Robert SpiderBoy'. When it asked for a photograph, he looked through the files on the computer and found that Geoff had stored some really nice ones, and some really weird ones too. So Robert ignored the weird ones and chose a nice one of a boy and then uploaded it. Then, just so he wouldn't seem too different to the other children, because he didn't want to put them off, he wrote a profile which was very similar to all the other

children. They seemed to know what to say, thought Robert, so I'll just copy them, and so he wrote this...

I'm Robert SpiderBoy.
I'm 10. I like hanging

out, footie, watching
TV.

The photo he had chosen made
him seem like a nice boy. It showed
the sun shining in the background, a
big toothy grin, a mop of black hair
and a dusting of freckles and he was
wearing a cool t-shirt. He looked very
nice. Goofy, happy, friendly,
outdoorsy, fun.

Satisfied with his profile, Robert
prepared to send his first
message and he decided to
send his first message to Kayden.

'Hi,' he wrote because that was
nice and simple to do. Then he
pressed send. Another message
appeared which said,

14

'Kayden must accept your friendship request before you can send him a message.'

So Robert sent him a friend request first. Then, Robert sat watching the screen waiting for a response. He could see that Kayden was online because he had a little green dot next to his photo and next to the green dot were the words…

Kayden is online now.

Then, Kayden's photo disappeared and another message popped up.

Kayden only accepts friendship requests from people he knows.

REJECTED

"Oh," said Robert, feeling deflated. "Why would he do that? Surely, a boy can never have too many friends." Robert felt rejected and sad. He did not, however, give up, and decided to increase his chances of making new friendships by sending friendship requests to as many children as he was allowed. Surely at least one child would accept him as a new friend.

16

So Robert began sending lots and lots and lots of friendship requests and before long he had sent them to more than two hundred children. He didn't really care if the children were handsome, or pretty, or cool, he just wanted one, anyone one, to be his friend.

Not long after the last friendship request was sent, Robert was delighted to see his friendship requests had been accepted by five children. Now he had five new friends. How jubilant he felt. His new friends were Peter, Becca, Madgirl, Frankie and FootieMonster.

Robert wasted no time writing and sending a new message to each of his new friends. It was the same message, copied and pasted to all of them in turn.

'Hi, I really like the look of your profile. You seem like such fun!' he sent, even though he hadn't read any of their profiles yet as he had just sent friendship requests to anyone.

Much to Robert's surprise and delight, each of the children sent him

a reply. For the first time in a long time, Robert no longer felt lonely.

Days, weeks and months passed by and, although Madgirl had stopped replying to Robert's messages, the other children hadn't, so Robert still had four friends. Furthermore, another two children had accepted his

18

friendship requests since, and another five who were friends of theirs. Robert felt positively popular and couldn't wait each day for the children to get home from school so that he could continue chatting with them about their day.

After another month or so had passed by, Robert had twenty 'friends', but only really chatted with FootieMonster, Becca, and a newer friend called Aidan. The other children ignored Robert's messages, even though they kept him as a 'friend,' which was better than nothing, Robert thought.

FootieMonster was mad about football, as you have probably guessed, and liked talking about it all the time, which didn't seem to annoy Robert as much as it did his other friends.

FOOTIE MONSTER

Becca was mad about make-up and liked posting selfies online, then talking about how good she looked in them all the time, which didn't seem to annoy Robert as much as it did her other friends.

Becca

Aidan didn't really like doing much at all and seemed a little depressed that no one liked him.

He sent messages that said things like this,

'Everyone hates me,'
'my family hate me,'
'my teachers hate me,'

'girls hate me,' 'boys hate me,' 'babies hate me,' and 'no one likes me,' all the time, which didn't seem to annoy Robert as much as it would have annoyed his other friends, if he he'd had any.

'I like you a lot,' typed Robert.

'Yeah, but no one likes me in real life I mean,' said Aidan, 'you don't count.'

'Well, I'm sure I would still like you in

23

real life,' said Robert, 'if we were ever to meet. That's how much I like you.'

'I don't think so,' said Aidan.

'I do think so,' replied Robert. 'Why don't you come over and we can find out if you are right, or if I am right.'

'Hm, I'm not sure. Where do you live?' asked Aidan.

'I live in a big house on top of a hill,' Robert replied.

'Is it really big?' asked Aidan.

'Yes,' replied Robert. 'It's a mansion.'

'Wow, are you rich?'

'I don't know. I've never thought about it,' replied Robert.

'Lucky you if you are,' said Aidan.

'Why don't you come round and see it, my

'I live in a big house on top of a hill,' Robert replied.

'Is it really big?' asked Aidan.

'Yes,' replied Robert. 'It's a mansion.'

'Wow, are you rich?'

'I don't know. I've never thought about it,' replied Robert.

'Lucky you if you are,' said Aidan.

'Why don't you come round and see it, my

house that is? You could come round for a playdate.' typed Robert hopefully. He knew other children had playdates, but had never ever had one of his own. It seemed Aidan had never had one either. Perhaps they could be the answer to each others dreams.

'A real playdate?' typed Aidan. 'Like meet up and have a playdate in real life?'

'Yeah, sure,' said Robert. 'Wouldn't it be fun?'

'Yes,' said Aidan. 'I think it would.'

'Your mum won't mind?' asked Robert.

'She hates me,' said Aidan. 'She hates me so much she's bound to say no. She'd hate me to have a friend.'

'Oh,' said Robert. 'That's a shame. Must you tell

28

her? Can't you just come on your own?'

'I suppose. Yeah.

Sure. I just won't tell her. She wont even notice; she hates me that much,' said Aidan.

'So does that mean you'll come?' said Robert hopefully.

'Yes, definintely. I'll come,' said Aidan.

So Robert gave Aidan his address and Aidan got three buses across town, and then he climbed the crooked hill all the way up to Robert's house. It was all just so exciting, to be going to a friend's house to play.

The next day Robert, who was gaining confidence now, sent Becca a message, 'would you like you like to come to my house for a playdate?' he asked.

'What, in real life?' she replied.

'Yeah,' said Robert. 'In real life.'

'I'm not supposed to meet people I don't know in real life,' said Becca.

'What's to know about me that you don't

already know?' said Robert. 'Except that my mum is a make-up buyer for a beauty company in Paris.'

'Is she?' said Becca.

'Yes,' said Robert. 'She knows all about make-up and has loads of free samples too. She'll probably let you have some and she knows people who are looking for models.'

'OMG,' said Becca, 'do you think she could make me a model?'

'Well, only if she meets you in real life,' said Robert.

'Okay, I'll come.' Becca replied, and after that she took four buses and a tram across town, before climbing up the crooked hill towards the house, even though she was starting to feel a little scared. "Well, of course a make-up buyer would have a big house like that," she said to herself, and continued on up because she really really really wanted to meet Robert's mum.

The next day after school, Robert sent a message to FootieMonster, because Becca and Aidan were offline.

'How you doin'?' typed Robert, trying to sound cool because he knew FootieMonster liked cool.

35

'I lost my game against Raven's school,' said FootieMonster despondently.

'Oh, too bad,' said Robert.

'Yeah, we should have won but the stoopid ref didn't spot Raven was offside when they scored the winning goal.'

'Hey, that's really too bad,' said Robert, who didn't really know much about football but he sensed that if he didn't keep talking about football, FootieMonster would lose interest and log off. 'My dad

36

would have had something to say about that.'

'Your dad? Is he a

ref?' said FootieMonster.

'No not a ref, he's the chief executive of the city football club,' replied Robert.

'Our city?'

'Yes,' said Robert. 'Would you like to

come over for a playdate?'

'Oh,' said FootieMonster uncertainly, 'I'm not supposed to meet people I've met on the internet.'

'Oh, I understand,' said Robert. 'It's just that you could meet my dad. You'd have lots to talk about and he could probably give you some free tickets for some games.'

'Does he know if there are any spaces in the junior team?' said FootieMonster.

'Yes, there are,' said Robert. 'You could talk to him about that and show him your football skills.'

'Wow,' replied FootieMonster. 'Wow. When shall I come?'

'You can come over now if you like,' replied Robert.

'Okay. I'm already on my way,' replied FootieMonster.

So, FootieMonster took a tram, four buses and a taxi to the bottom of the crooked hill.

As he stood at the bottom and looked up he felt a bit scared, but knew he would always regret not taking the chance to meet the chief executive of the city football club in person.

He might even get a ticket to the city cup final. So off Footie monster

went. He climbed up the hill so fast

he was puffing and panting by the time he reached the front door, which was open. FootieMonster stepped inside the house. He was in a large hallway which looked as though it hadn't been cleaned in a long time and it made FootieMonster unsure.

Then again, he thought, it was a big house, a mansion in fact, just the kind of house (if you forget about the dust and the dead flies and the cobwebs everywhere) that a chief executive of a city football club would live in. A sign on another door, written in scrawly handwriting said, 'This way FootieMonster,' and an arrow pointed though the door.

So FootieMonster followed the arrow and began opening the door, just as the front door, caught by a breeze perhaps, slammed shut behind him.

FootieMonster slowly pushed the door open, and as he walked into the room, which was very dark, he seemed to get caught in something ropey, like a net, which also happened to be very sticky.

It stuck to the hair on his arms, so that he couldn't set them free

without pulling his hair out. It stuck
to his cheeks and his nose and the
hair on his head. The more he
struggled, the more bits of him got
stuck to the net.

"Urgh!" he said at first,
thinking he would be
free in no time, before
quickly realising he was getting more
and more stuck, and the net was
getting tighter and tighter.

"Help, help!"

And then, when he had
exhausted himself trying to get free,
when in fact all he had done was
make the net tighter, he began to sob.

"Robert!" he called, "Robert,
where are you? I can't escape!"

45

But the next voice he heard wasn't Robert's, it was a girl, and she said:

"None of us can."

"What?" said FootieMonster.

"None of us can escape," said the girl, who happened to be Becca.

Then he heard another voice, the voice of a boy. "It was a trap," said Aidan. "We've been tricked and now we're stuck here forever in these nets."

As FootieMonster's eyes grew more accustomed to the dim light, he could see two other children hanging from the ceiling, wrapped up in what looked like big cobwebs.

"Are you Robert?" FootieMonster asked.

46

"No. My name is Aiden. Robert tricked us. He's tricked us all."

"Robert," called FootieMonster. "Robert let us go at once or else!" he added bravely, and he shook and shook the big cobweb with all his might as he tried to break out of it.

"I'm coming!" he heard another voice reply. **47**

"Robert, is that you?" said FootieMonster.

"Yes, it's me," said Robert, "and try not to worry. Remember I am your friend."

"It's just a joke," FootieMonster, said to Aidan. "You'll see," he said hopefully. "He'll let us go in a minute and we'll all have a right laugh."

"I'm coming," said Robert, and there was a scratching, then a scuttling noise from some where in the room that they couldn't see. FootieMonster swung around to see if Robert was coming in through the door, but he wasn't, so he swung around to see if Robert was coming through the window, but he wasn't, so he swung around to see if he was coming down the chimney and into the fireplace, but he wasn't. "Where are you, I cant see you?" said FootieMonster.

"Why I'm here," said Robert, and an enormous hairy spider descended

49

from the ceiling on a web. It was as big as a car and most certainly was not a goofy boy with freckles at all. It most certainly did not have glamorous parents, or any kind of parents at all.

"Hi!" said Robert, waggling his long hairy front legs in FootieMonster's face.

"Oh, I'm so happy girl and boys, because now that I have caught you forever in my web, I'll never ever feel lonely again."

The end

Questionnaire.

This questionnaire has been devised to consolidate your understanding of the text and to facilitate discussion around internet safety.

The questionnaire can be completed by readers individually, or as a group and class discussion.

Answers are given on a separate page at the back.

Multiple choice (please choose 1 answer per question)

1. Why do you think Robert lied about being a boy?

a/ Because he wanted to be one.

b/ To make the children trust him and like him more.

c/ Because he didn't like girls.

51

Your answer

....

2. Why did Kayden only accept requests from people he knew?

a/ Because he was being mean.

b/ Because he didn't want new friends.

c/ Because he knows that strangers on the internet might not be safe.

Your answer

....

3. You shouldn't share too much personal information online. What did Robert do with the information the children shared with him?

a/ Made fun of their hobbies and bullied them.

b/ Nothing.

c/ Used it to lie about his own life so that the children would like to meet up with him.

Your answer

....

4.If you get a friendship request from someone you don't know, what should you do?

a/ Delete or block them and tell your parents or an adult you trust.

b/ Accept it but never talk to them.

c/ Ask your friends if they know who they are, if they've spoken to them then they must be safe.

Your answer

....

5. Is a stranger on the internet safer than a stranger in the street?

a/ Yes.

b/ No.

c/ It depends.

Your answer

....

Short answer questions

6. Why do you think Madgirl stopped replying to Robert's messages?

53

Your answer

....

....

....

....

7. Look at your answer to question 6. Why was this a good thing for her to do?

Your answer

....

....

....

....

8. Why do you think Robert wanted to talk to the other children every day?

Your answer

....

....

....

....

9. Why did Robert encourage Aiden not to tell his mum about meeting up with him?

Your answer

....

....

....

....

10. How was Robert able to trick the children into coming to his house?

Your answer

....

....

....

....

11. Why did Robert make the children come to his house rather than go out?

Your answer

....

....

....

....

12. If a stranger approached you in real life, what would you do?

Your answer

....

....

....

....

13. Look at your answer to question 11. If a stranger approached you on the internet, what would you do?

Your answer

....

....

....

....

Longer answer questions

14. Why do you think people tend to trust people they meet online? Why is this a bad thing?

Your answer

....

....

....

....

....

....

....

....

15. If you were FootieMonster, Madgirl or Aiden, what would you have done better to keep yourself safe from someone like Robert?

Your answer

....

....

....

....

....

....

....

....

16. Should you worry about a person's feelings if you block them or delete them from contacting you?

Your answer

....

....

....

....

....

....

....

....

Please find the answers on the following pages.

BUT FIRST READ THIS.....

If you are chatting online to someone that you don't know please tell a parent or teacher, or another trusted adult NOW, even if you think the person seems nice.

Please call CHILDLINE on Call 0800 1111 if you are worried about anything that is happening to you online and do not feel like you have anyone else to tell.

That's CHILDLINE 0800 1111

If you are unsure how to discuss your worries with a trusted adult, why not bring along this book, or mention that you have read it and what it's about and you can explain what is happening to you from there.

Answers

1/ b 2/ c 3/ c 4/ a 5/ b

Sample short answers

6/ Madgirl realised she should not be friends with a stranger she did not know.

7/ It was a good thing because it meant Robert could no longer contact her and trick her into coming to his house. By blocking him she kept herself safe.

8/ Robert wanted to talk to the children every day so that he could get to know more and more about them until they completely trusted him. Robert was grooming the children.

9/ Robert persuaded Aiden not to tell his mum because he knew his mum would stop Aiden from coming.

10/ He lied to each child about his own life. So, Robert knew Aiden needed a best friend because Aiden told him he was so lonely. He knew Becca loved make-up so he tricked her by pretending his mum was a make-up buyer for a beauty company in Paris. With FootieMonster, Robert pretended his dad was the manager of the city football club. These were all lies.

11/ Robert knew he could trap the children in his own house. If they met in public the children could run away, or cry for help but once they were in his house they were trapped.

12/ Run away and tell a teacher or parent what happened.

13/ Block or delete them and tell a teacher or parent what happened.

Sample Longer answers

14/ People tend to trust people online because it is easier for people online to lie about who they are. They can use fake names and fake photos to trick us into believing they are someone nice and someone like us.
Without knowing them from school, or through family, it's impossible to know if strangers are telling the truth.
They can use information we give them to pretend they are like us and have the same interests as us which makes us think they are nice and trustworthy, when in fact they are lying and might be someone dangerous.

15/ If I were any of those children, I would have blocked Robert straightaway and I would have told my parents about him. I might even tell my teacher incase the same person is trying to contact any of my friends.
If I block this person straightaway they cannot trick me or lie to me at all, so I don't have to worry about whether they are safe or not.

61

16/ No. I should never worry about hurting someone's feelings if I block them. I am allowed to do this to keep myself safe. I have complete control over who I let talk to me and if they are strangers, or make me feel bad in any way I can and will block them. It is more important for me to be safe than to worry about someone else's feelings.

Look out for our new spine tingling tale coming soon...

WIN THIS DAD COMPETITION

How would you like to win this dad for 1 week?

-Want to swim with dolphins?
-No problem.

-Want to be driven around in a fleet of luxury cars?
-No problem.

-Want to live in a mansion?
-No problem.

-Want to be seen around with the handsomest man in the world?
-No problem.

BUY YOUR RAFFLE TICKET TODAY
FOR YOUR LAST CHANCE TO
WIN THIS DAD

Other books from Jimkins Publishing include our Genius baby range

Printed in Great Britain
by Amazon